KAFKA IN 90 MINUTES

Kafka

IN 90 MINUTES

Paul Strathern

IVAN R. DEE
CHICAGO

Library of Congress Cataloging-in-Publication Data:
Strathern, Paul, 1940–
    Kafka in 90 minutes / Paul Strathern.
        p. cm. — (Great writers in 90 minutes)
    Includes bibliographical references and index.
    ISBN 1-56663-621-3 (alk. paper) —
    ISBN 1-56663-620-5 (pbk. : alk. paper)
    1. Kafka, Franz, 1883–1924. 2. Kafka, Franz, 1883–1924—
Criticism and interpretation. 3. Authors, Austrian—20th
century—Biography. I. Title: Kafka in ninety minutes. II. Title.

PT2621.A26Z89434 2004
833'.912—dc22
                                                      2004052725

Contents

KAFKA IN 90 MINUTES

Introduction

On October 23, 1902, the nineteen-year-old Franz Kafka attended a talk given at the German University of Prague by a fellow student called Max Brod. The talk was entitled "Schopenhauer and Nietzsche," with Brod insisting that Nietzsche was a "fraud." This so provoked Kafka that he overcame his habitual shyness and approached Brod after his talk.

As they walked home through the streets of Prague, their argument turned into a discussion. They quickly discovered that they shared a deep interest in literature and an ambivalent attitude toward their mutual Jewishness. This was the beginning of a friendship that would continue

7

throughout Kafka's life—and beyond. Brod would become Kafka's closest and only genuinely intimate friend. He would also, in a totally unforeseen way, become Kafka's savior.

Kafka and Brod made an incongruous pair. Kafka was a darkly handsome young man, tall and thin, often dressed in an elegant blue suit, which in the words of Brod was "as unobtrusive and reserved as himself." Brod, on the other hand, was a short, ebullient hunchback whose deformed body was crowned by an oversized head. Although only in his first year at university, Brod had already established himself as a wunderkind. He wrote poetry and had announced that he was to become a writer; he was a considerable pianist and composed music; and he already spoke several languages. Despite his unprepossessing appearance, he had also established himself as a tireless womanizer. Kafka, for his part, was a second-year student but appeared to have no idea what he was or what he wanted to become. He had entered the university to study chemistry but had abandoned this subject after two weeks. He had then enrolled to study

8

"Germanistics," a general course embracing the German language, literature, and culture. But he had quickly become disenchanted with the attitude of German triumphalism adopted by his lecturers, and had abandoned this too. According to Brod, "Law he took up with a sigh because it was the school that involved the least fixed goal, or the largest choice of goals—that is to say, the school that put off longest taking a decision and anyhow didn't demand any great preference." Kafka's opinion of his law studies was as disenchanted as ever: "Intellectually I fed myself exclusively on sawdust—sawdust, too, which had already been chewed by thousands of jaws before me."

After graduating from university, Kafka worked as a legal adviser to an insurance company while attempting to write at night and in his spare time. Becoming more and more reclusive, he began to exhibit increasing weakness of character. Along with his indecisiveness, he developed all manner of hypochondriac complaints, suffering from insomnia as well as a chronic inability to assert himself. Yet alongside these defects he exhibited an extraordinary strength. He developed the uncanny ability to observe himself with cool objectivity, and cultivated this ability in his writing, where it manifested itself in increasingly original metaphorical form. His most characteristic and telling work was the story "Metamorphosis," which opens with the words:

> Gregor Samsa woke one morning from a night of troubled dreams to discover that he had become transformed into a large insect. He was lying on his hard, so to speak armor-plated, back and when he lifted his head a little he could see his domelike brown belly divided into corrugated segments, which the bed quilt barely covered and was about to slide off completely. His numerous legs, which were pitifully thin compared to the rest of his bulk, waved helplessly before his eyes.
>
> What has happened to me? He wondered. It was no dream. His room, a regular human bedroom, though rather small, lay quiet within its four familiar walls.

As the years went by, Kafka's self-loathing increased. Unable to bring himself to marry or abandon his job, he began suffering from persistently debilitating anorexia, and his hypochondria was now accompanied by genuine illnesses. He continued to write, at great psychological cost, but remained a virtual failure. By contrast, his friend Max Brod went from success to success, producing novels at the rate of more than one a year, achieving international renown, and despite getting married continued to become embroiled in a succession of romantic affairs. His ability to speak Czech, a language belittled by the German-speaking inhabitants of Czechoslovakia, led him to champion the Czech writer Jaroslav Hasek, promoting his subversive comic masterpiece *The Good Soldier Schweik*, a precursor of *Catch-22* set in the Austro-Hungarian Army during the First World War. Brod's musical expertise led him to publicize the work of the little-known composer Leos Janacek, now widely regarded as the leading Czech composer of his generation. At the same time Brod never forgot his dear friend Kafka, though his efforts at promoting Kafka's work achieved very little. Despite Brod's literary success, and his high opinion of himself, he began to suspect—and declare publicly—that the work of his neurotically diffident friend was better than his own, and indeed was superior to any being published in the German language. This was generous acclaim for a completely unknown writer, living in a provincial backwater, during one of the major periods of German literature—whose currently acknowledged stars included the likes of Thomas Mann and Rainer Maria Rilke, Hermann Hesse and Bertolt Brecht.

By 1922 Kafka had become pathologically secretive and beset by angst. In despair over his life, his writing, and his self-destructive ways, he saw himself as fated to "a battle of annihilation." He concluded: "My scribbling . . . is nothing more than my own materialization of horror. . . . It should be burnt." In this state of mind, with his body now succumbing to tuberculosis, he wrote to Brod:

> Dear Max, perhaps this time I won't get up again, after the month of pulmonary fever the

onset of pneumonia is likely enough, and writing this down, though it has some power, won't keep it away. . . .

He went on to send Brod "my last will for everything I've written." Of all his writings, he considered just half a dozen printed pieces "valid." But these were never to be reprinted and should be allowed to "disappear completely." As for the rest:

> everything else I've written (in periodicals, papers, manuscripts or letters) is without exception, insofar as it can be obtained or recovered from the adressees . . . all this is without exception to be burnt, preferably unread (I won't stop you from looking at it, I'd like it best of all if you didn't, but in any case nobody else must see it)—I ask you to burn it all as soon as possible—

Two years later, at the age of just forty, Kafka died of tuberculosis. Brod found himself in a quandary. He believed deeply in Kafka's writing, but he had given his deeply beloved friend a solemn promise. Fortunately for posterity, Brod decided to break it.

Yet this was not all. Brod eventually succeeded in securing the publication of one after another of Kafka's works. One by one these works passed virtually unnoticed. Brod then went to all the trouble of writing a long and detailed biography of his great friend, which was published in Prague in 1937. A year later the Nazis invaded Czechoslovakia, and in the ensuing years of the Second World War the German-Jewish culture of central Europe (*mitteleuropa*) disappeared in the Holocaust. Brod would manage to escape to Israel, where after the war he continued tirelessly publicizing Kafka's work in the midst of writing his own. This would have an ironic result. By the time of Brod's death in 1968, his oeuvre consisted of some seventy-five full-length books as well as literally thousands of articles, poems, and essays. Yet by then these were largely forgotten. Max Brod was internationally famous only because of his biography of Franz Kafka and his unstinting promotion of his long-dead friend.

Kafka's Life and Works

Franz Kafka was born on July 3, 1883, in Prague, which was then a provincial city in the Austro-Hungarian Empire.

Prague, like Dublin and Alexandria, two other provincial cities on the periphery of Europe, would produce a disproportionate number of great twentieth-century writers. Besides Kafka, Prague was home to German poet Rilke, the playwright Franz Werfel, and Hasek. (Alexandria produced the Italian poet Giuseppe Ungaretti, the Futurist Emilio Marinetti, and the Greek poet C. P. Cavafy, while Dublin produced George Bernard Shaw, Oscar Wilde, James Joyce, and Samuel Beckett. Several capital cities produced less.) The factors contributing to this phenomenon appear to have been an independent provincial life with intellectually thriving minority populations. In the case of Prague, a largely middle-class German-speaking minority kept itself culturally apart from the indigenous Czech population. Kafka was further marginalized by being a Jew within this German-speaking community. Anti-Semitism was rife throughout the Austro-Hungarian Empire, especially among the German-speaking people, and a strong undercurrent of quasi-racial alienation would be a persistent feature of Kafka's life and work.

Another formative influence in Kafka's life was his father, the formidable Hermann Kafka, who ran a prosperous fancy-goods shop at the Kinsky Palace, which faced the Old Town Square. Like so much in Kafka's life, his father was a paradoxical figure—both very much a part of the Jewish family past, yet at the same time breaking free from it. Hermann's father Jakob, Franz Kafka's grandfather, had been a Yiddish-speaking butcher, the second son of nine children who all grew up in a single-room wooden hut in

the village of Wossek, deep in the Czech countryside. A tough character, he was said to have
been able to lift a sack of flour with his teeth. An
earlier anti-Semitic law had forbidden any but
the eldest sons to marry and have children, but
this measure was rescinded when Jakob was
thirty-six. He then married and had six children,
one of whom was Hermann, and they were all
brought up in dire poverty in the family hut. As
Hermann was fond of proclaiming in later life,
this large family subsisted mostly on a diet of po-
tatoes, when these were available, and on nothing when they were not.

Young Hermann was soon put to work
pulling the family cart, delivering slabs of meat,
often tramping through miles of snow to distant
homesteads in the woods. As a result, he suffered
from frostbite and footsores. Years later, despite
being a prosperous merchant, he delighted in
showing off his scars before his sensitive son
Franz. Hermann grew up to become a burly, ro-
bust character, a man who believed in hard work
and no nonsense. After three years of military
service in the Austrian army, during which he rose

to become a sergeant, he became a peddler, selling goods throughout the Czech lands, finally earning enough to open a shop in Prague. Going about his business there, he experienced less than the usual anti-Semitism for the simple fact that he did not look like a Jew, did not conduct himself like one, and paid only lip service to the Jewish religion.

Kafka would always be inordinately aware of his role as the oldest son, yet clearly he did not take to it naturally. To such a figure as Hermann, the spindly and bookish young weakling who was growing up to become his son and heir was a continual source of irritation. Hermann did his best to cajole and bully the young Franz into some semblance of normality during his school-days, but to no avail. Franz was not to be normalized. He simply became even more sensitive and took to keeping to himself. In the course of his childhood, Franz's already astute mind developed its own inner resources to an exceptional degree. He appeared weak, and he was aware that he appeared weak, but this clear-sighted self-awareness proved little but a torment. As we have seen, this faculty would later become ingrained: his writing would make use of it—which had the curious effect both of alleviating the immediate torment and making him even more painfully aware of himself.

Kafka had three sisters—the middle one, Ottla, became his favorite—and they too were not spared the attentions of their domineering father. Even in public, Hermann was not above reproaching his children, remonstrating with them about what they should have been but could not be. Yet in many ways Hermann appeared to others as the epitome of bluff normality, a successful businessman and a good provider for his family. This too inevitably had its double-edged effect on his family. For Kafka and his sisters, living with their father was a constant trial. On occasion the siblings would gather secretively in the bathroom to work out what to say in their defense. But to no avail: this was a trial in which they were inescapably guilty. Naturally (not a word that immediately springs to mind with reference to Kafka), this family atmosphere built up in him an enormous reservoir of guilt. Here, at least partly, was the source of his future self-loathing.

There is no denying that Kafka's childhood and inherent weaknesses rendered him a psychological mess, prey to all manner of neuroses. Yet one must constantly bear in mind that in many ways he overcame, and made great positive use of, these neuroses in later life. And besides seeing himself very clearly, he also learned to laugh at himself. Max Brod constantly testified to how much the two of them laughed together. The darkness of Kafka's life, and his creations, were frequently illuminated by lightning flashes of the absurd. He was never less than aware of the ridiculousness of his situation. Among many other things, he was also a survivor.

Such survival, and the creation he made of it, bespeaks a deep tenuous strength which lived alongside his constantly debilitating weakness. This strength both disguised his weakness and enabled him to examine it more closely. Kafka's weakness was far from visible—to anyone but his father, who would probably have found any son of his inadequate. Even as he grew up, Kafka learned to present a public face of extreme normality, which he maintained at all times. Yet this was a minor creation compared with the literary works that he learned to draw out of himself, like a snake emerging from its skin. Many people are neurotic, with greater or lesser reason, yet how many manage to recreate their neuroses in such consummate artistic form? Kafka's imagination would create the fable of his life, from his childhood onward. And like so many childhood fables, this "life fable" would feature many more or less humanized animals. To escape from the misery of his being, Kafka began early on to imagine himself as an animal, characterizing his being with animaline qualities. As we have seen, Kafka would most famously identify himself with an insect, the beetle hero of "Metamorphosis." At other times in his stories he would identify with a rodent, a dog, a mouse, even an ape—all of them despised creatures in their own way. Yet for Kafka these animals were not portrayed as despicable in themselves, only in the eyes of others, or in their own eyes.

In one very particular way, this identifying with animals was with Kafka from the outset. A century earlier the Jews of the Austro-Hungarian

Empire had been ordered to take on surnames. Unlike Jewish names, these had to be Europeanized and comprehensible to the authorities. In practice, the visiting government officials often simply gave the Jews their names, handing them out as they saw fit—sometimes serendipitously, often maliciously. Franz's ancestors had been given the name Kafka, which meant "crow." The young, dark-complexioned Kafka, with his delicate birdlike features and beaky nose, would certainly have been made aware of his crowlike qualities at school—if not by his Jewish classmates, then certainly by the German pupils.

Compared with Hermann, Kafka's mother Julie (née Löwy) remains a somewhat enigmatic figure. She certainly had her weakness, invariably capitulating to her husband, even taking his side against the children in order to deflect any aggression from herself. Surreptitiously, she could be more sympathetic to Franz and his sisters. Julie spent much of her time away working in the family shop, selling gloves, hosiery, and umbrellas to the middle-class clientele. The children were looked after by a maid until she came home in the evening. Kafka would remember fondly how her arrival "causes the day, already so late, to begin again." He reflected "how comforting mother can be," yet characteristically remembered, "I did not always love my mother as she deserved and as I could, only because the German language prevented it. The Jewish mother is no 'Mutter' [the German word for mother] . . . we give a Jewish woman the name of a German mother, but forget the contradiction that sinks into the emotions so much the more heavily." Kafka was being disingenuous here: the causes of his inadequate feelings toward his mother were certainly more than linguistic. Yet his very sensitivity, accompanied by his constant searching for an answer to his problems, any answer, caused him to unearth and examine all manner of insights.

In attempting to assimilate, the German Jews spoke the language of a people from whom they often felt alien, a people who frequently despised them. Kafka was one of the first to pinpoint this inextricable predicament, whose full force would become apparent after the Second World War in the poetry of the great German-speaking Jewish poet Paul Celan. Kafka was aware that the very language he wrote in was somehow not "natural" to him. His endlessly analytic style coolly set down, but never expressed emotionally, the anger and bewilderment he felt at his own situation. When Gregor Samsa awakes and finds that he has metamorphosed into a large insect, he does not rage at what has happened, instead he examines every aspect of it and what he is going to do about it. When his mother knocks on the door to get him up, "Gregor wanted to answer at length and explain everything, but in the circumstances he confined himself to saying, 'Yes, yes, thank you, mother, I'm getting up now.'" Even amidst this monstrous abnormality, he wishes to remain normal, somehow to resolve his situation by thinking about it. "His immediate intention was to get up quietly without being disturbed, to put on his clothes and above all eat his breakfast, and only then to consider what else was to be done, since in bed, he was well aware, his meditations would come to no sensible conclusion."

Kafka's mother Julie came from the Löwy family, who were more varied and much more intellectually developed than the Kafkas. Julie's grandfather had been a rabbi, who had been regarded by many as a saint. He had also been a renowned scholar of the Talmud, the book of the laws that govern Jewish Orthodox behavior, along with commentaries and interpretations of these laws. Interpretation of the Talmud had for many generations provided intellectual grist for the finest Jewish minds, often in deprived rural circumstances where such minds could have found no other outlet. This activity, though essentially arid and unproductive, had done much to preserve and develop the Jewish intellect. Indeed, Talmudic study in many ways accounts for the astonishing Jewish contribution to European intellectual life that began in the mid-nineteenth century and achieved its finest flowering throughout the twentieth. Before this time, few Jews had achieved intellectual eminence in European thought. The shining exception is the seventeenth-century Dutch-Jewish philosopher Baruch Spinoza, who had indicatively been excommunicated from Judaism. But as soon as the Jews of Europe began to assimilate and exercise their intellect on other than Talmudic matters, the results were remarkable. Instead of abstract religious argumentation, brilliant Jewish minds now applied themselves to secular abstractions, especially mathematics and theoretical physics. Einstein was but the greatest of a host of great twentieth-century theoretical scientists who were Jewish. (From Niels Bohr to John von Neumann, from J. Robert Oppenheimer to Richard Feynman, the list is seemingly endless.) Jews also began to flourish in other fields—from law to finance, from literature to art. Kafka's achievement in literature was accompanied by that of Arnold Schoenberg in music, Marc Chagall in painting, and a flowering throughout the cultural field. It would thus seem no accident that Kafka's ancestor on the Löwy side of the family, the saintly Amschel (Adam), was a renowned and revered Talmudic scholar. And, as we shall see, the unending legalistic and procedural complications of Talmudic scholarship would have a particular echo in Kafka's works, especially in his two best-known novels, *The Trial* and *The Castle*.

Kafka's great-grandfather Amschel may have been a saint, but living with a saint in the family was not easy. His wife committed suicide, and his son became insane. Other members of the Löwy family went a variety of different ways. Franz's Löwy grandfather had run a brewery in Prague while Franz's bachelor uncle Alfred became a director of a company that ran Spanish railways; and his uncle Siegfried, who also remained a bachelor, lived a solitary, secretive life as a country doctor. Siegfried's general oddity endeared him to his young nephew, though his equally odd uncle Rudolf, who converted to Christianity and hid himself away as a clerk in a Prague brewery, proved less of an attraction.

There can be no doubt that Kafka inherited many traits from the Löwy side of his family, while it is possible that his mental tenacity was the legacy of his ebullient and determinedly philistine father. With hindsight it is easy to pinpoint such family traits, though the extent of their formative role in Kafka's extremely complex personality remains problematic. Many of the confidently Freudian interpretations of Kafka, which abounded during the high tide of psycho-analysis, have begun to look distinctly obsessive and shaky now that Freud's existence as a scientific investigator has given way to the picture of him as a rampant mythologizer. With this in view, it is better now to look upon Kafka's heritage of difficult saintliness, suicide, and a minor railway magnate as raw material facts rather than as the ingredients for abstruse theories.

Like so many of us, Kafka presented himself in public as a resolutely normal human being. Until such time as he developed and expanded upon his neuroses in his later literary work, we should give him the benefit of the doubt where appearances are concerned. With this in mind, we can have little difficulty in accepting Kafka as a very normal adolescent, who like so many of his kind had difficulty in accepting the boorishness and insensibility of their hardworking fathers. He escaped from the oppressive atmosphere at home by taking long walks through the atmospheric streets of Prague's Alstadt (the central old city district). Atop the hill on the far side of the river, the spires and grim façade of Hradcany (Prague Castle) brooded over the rooftops. At night he immersed himself in books, escaping into the vivid world of imagination. He read long and widely, but found himself particularly drawn to the meticulous prose of Flaubert, who eschewed analysis for the perfection of surface description. He also found himself attracted to the early short works of Thomas Mann, which spoke of the utter dedication required of the artist, who must forsake marriage and the joys of an ordinary life for the spiritual solitude of the creator.

Kafka's school reports spoke of a moderately bright pupil who did not appear exceptional in any way. His fellow pupils found him friendly enough but noted his ultimate reserve. This was the disitinctly normal student who at eighteen confidently took up his place at the German University of Prague. It was the inner, reserved character who dithered indecisively—deciding to study chemistry, then after two weeks deciding that he would be better off studying Germanistics, only to find this not to his taste, instead deciding to study law, which he knew was not to his taste but which allowed him to keep more options open, so that when he graduated he could then decide what he really wanted to do, or what he really didn't want to do.

By now Kafka had begun to entertain the vague idea that he might become a writer, or perhaps an artist. This was encouraged by his friendship with Max Brod, who declared his own ambition with no reserve, showing his latest stories and poems to Kafka. In response, Kafka began writing short pieces of his own, and also began to produce strange sketches. These frequently featured matchstick figures, in awkward poses, peculiarly evocative of isolation, ennui, and angst. Kafka described these to Brod as "purely personal, and therefore illegible hieroglyphs." When Brod had a book of poems accepted by a publisher, he loyally suggested one of Kafka's drawings for the cover. But this was deemed by the publisher to be "not reproducible." Despite this setback, Brod remained convinced of Kafka's artistic talent, even informing some artists he knew: "I can tell you the name of a very great artist—Franz Kafka."

Kafka graduated in 1906 and was now faced with the prospect of choosing a career. Possibly through direct pressure from his father, certainly through pressure that he imagined his father to be putting on him, Kafka decided to embark upon a career in the law—the one thing that he knew he did not want to do. To fulfill his professional requirements he became a judge's clerk at the courts. This post, which was more in the nature of an assistant, involved attending the hearings by the examining judges and taking notes of the proceedings. Despite having studied the law, this experience of its actual practice proved an eye-opener to the innocent young graduate. His legal studies enabled him to understand the proceedings and the jargon-ridden legalistic exchanges between the judge and the lawyers, but it soon became clear to him that the one person who did not understand what was going on was the defendant. Each officer of the judiciary performed his covert role in the proceedings while the defendant merely occupied the role of unwitting victim.

31

Despite the long and tiresome hours of work, Kafka was determined to continue with his writing. After the court sittings, he would painstakingly write up his reports. Only when these were finished would he turn to his own writings, usually in the early hours of the night, when the family apartment was at last quiet and he could work undisturbed. Kafka's personality was ideally suited to making a conscientious, sober, and objective record of what had taken place in the courts, and this style was adapted with little difficulty to the very different material of his imaginative writing.

It was around this time that Kafka began his first short novel, entitled tellingly *Description of a Struggle*. This uneven piece contains several intimations of Kafka's later work. Its realistic opening adopts a deceptively matter-of-fact style:

> At about midnight a few people rose, bowed, shook hands, said it had been a pleasant evening, and then passed through the wide doorway into the vestibule, to put on their coats. The hostess stood in the middle of the

room and made graceful bowing movements, causing the dainty folds in her skirt to move up and down.

The first-person narrator also introduces himself in a similar, almost objective manner:

> I sat at a tiny table—it had three curved, thin legs—sipping my third glass of benedictine, and while I drank I surveyed my little store of pastry which I had myself picked out and arranged in a pile.

Like Kafka, he is tall and thin, and suffers from a certain self-loathing with regard to his appearance. The narrator leaves the party with an acquaintance, and they walk through the snow-covered streets into the night, ostensibly on their way to climb a local mountain. Their conversation is inconsequential, but as they continue along, the narrative becomes increasingly fantastical and dreamlike.

The next section of the novel, entitled "Diversions *or* proof that it's impossible to live," continues with the dreamlike sequence of events.

The narrator imagines that he is riding on the back of his acquaintance as if he were a horse: "by digging my fists into his back I urged him into a trot." When his acquaintance collapses, he abandons him. "I left him there on the stones without much regret and whistled down a few vultures which, obediently and with serious beaks, settled down on him." The narrator passes through strange landscapes which he seems to control: "Since, as a pedestrian I dreaded the effort of climbing the mountainous road, I let it become gradually flatter, let it slope down into a valley in the distance. The stones vanished at my will and the wind disappeared." There follows a dream within a dream, involving a mysterious yellow fat man who is carried on a litter through an oriental landscape (resembling the Japanese woodcuts that were so popular in Prague at the time), and various other fantasy scene shifts. The narrative eventually returns to the reality of the two acquaintances walking along the road.

As in so many dreams, the material in *Description of a Struggle* has many elements of dis-

guised autobiography, containing oblique refer-
ences to Kafka's fears and anxieties. The novel is
for the most part fitted more to the imagination
of a dream than the convincing imagination of a
literary narrative. Kafka was trying to say too
much—mainly about himself. Beneath the complex surface of a narrative only loosely anchored
to reality lies the simple fact of Kafka's being,
with all its troubles. This was a mistake that he
would quickly recognize, and it would prove in-
structive. His later technique would brilliantly
reverse this style, presenting a deceptively simple
surface beneath which lay undercurrents of be-
wildering complexity. *Description of a Struggle*
is very much an apprentice piece, though Brod
evidently thought otherwise. In a review of a
play for a Berlin magazine, he generously placed
the unpublished Kafka alongside three stars of
the German literary scene, Heinrich Mann,
Frank Wedekind, and Gustav Meyrink, singling
out Kafka for his lucidly meticulous style. This
was of course a preposterous comparison at the
time, though in the light of history Brod's prescience concerning his friend seems no less than

miraculous. The meticulousness, if not the plausibility, of Kafka's style is possibly the sole redeeming grace of *Description of a Struggle*.

Kafka spent the summer of 1907 at Triesch, staying with his uncle Siegfried, the doctor. Here he appears to have lapsed into the pleasant normality of a twenty-four-year-old bachelor enjoying a holiday in the country. He swam, sunbathed in the grass, and even rode around on a motorbike (a very modern and distinctly daring adventure in those days). During the evenings he played billiards and drank beer. He also spent a lot of time with two young women, describing them in a letter to Max Brod as "very bright girls, students, very keen Social Democrats" (that is, progressive thinkers). One was called Hedwig, and she was:

> small, with cheeks that are invariably red all over. She's very shortsighted—not merely as an excuse for her pretty gesture of adjusting spectacles on her nose, whose tip is really beautifully composed of tiny facets. Tonight I dreamed of her short, plump legs, and in

these roundabout ways I recognize the beauty of a girl and fall in love.

Hedwig lived in Vienna, and on his return to Prague, Kafka began corresponding with her, writing long love letters interspersed with characteristic remarks about himself. These were not just modest, deprecating remarks: as well as telling Hedwig how much he loved her, he also informed her that he was an "evil person." This established what was to become a lifelong habit in his relationships with women. He wanted them to love him, yet he wanted to prevent them from loving him. He wanted to be in love, yet he was afraid to surrender his feelings in this way. He wanted to share his life with someone, yet he felt sure that he would be unable to stand such constant proximity to another human being. Kafka decided that he wanted to speak Spanish, and he would come to learn it in Vienna, so that he could be near Hedwig. But why did he want to learn Spanish? So that he could travel to Spain where his uncle Alfred would find him a job in his railway company, or if there was no vacancy he could travel to look for work "in South America or the Azores." Amidst all this dithering, Hedwig announced that she wished to come and live in Prague, which disconcerted him. Kafka's holiday romance eventually petered out amidst a welter of misunderstandings.

In October, Kafka entered into permanent employment, embarking upon a career in the legal department of the Assicurazioni Generali, an Italian insurance company whose head office was in Trieste. He was now required to work more than ten hours a day, and in the evenings he began studying Italian, hoping this would enable him to be transferred to Trieste. He now had practically no time for writing, or even for meditating upon the problems of his situation and what he did or did not want to do with his life—the only two activities in which he appeared to be really interested. He scarcely had any time even to see his friend Max Brod, and wrote to him: "If my troubles previously walked on their feet, they are now, aptly, walking on their hands." Kafka was increasingly aware of the absurdity of his life, but when writing to Brod he also recognized the humorous side of his situation. This need to dress up his weakness in order to make it acceptable to others eliminated the element of self-pity and provided Kafka with a suitable literary guise. On the surface, he was always easily influenced. Feeling the need to live up to Brod's high opinion of his writing was to prove one of his most fruitful influences.

After nine months, Kafka's first attempt at permanent employment came to an abrupt end, and he left the Assicurazioni Generali; according to the company records, the reason for his resignation was "enervation connected with extreme cardiac excitablity." Despite this, he immediately took up another permanent position, this time in the legal department of the Workers' Accident Insurance Institute, a quasi-governmental organization. Here his duties at first proved less onerous, and he finished work at two in the afternoon. Thoughts of settling in Spain, the Azores, Latin America, or Trieste were abandoned, and he sublimated such dreams into his literary imaginings, writing long into the early hours in the family apartment when everyone else had gone to bed. But this was no easy matter, and Kafka soon began suffering from insomnia. As the ever-solicitous Brod described it:

> Kafka tried sleeping in the afternoon and writing at night. That always went all right for a certain length of time, but he was not getting his proper sleep—Franz suffered from poor sleep, and an unusual sensitivity to noise anyhow—conditions of exhaustion set in, and so he had to call upon his last reserves to get through his work in the office.

Kafka's need to write was becoming ever more clear to him as his life sank deeper into a futility of unfulfilment and weakness. His writing seemed to be the only thing that made his worthless life worthwhile. Regardless of his physical weakness, his health, even his fragile mental sensibilities, Kafka would continue to write. His dedication to this task soon ran beyond the realms of obstinacy, fulfilling some ultimate spiritual need. As he himself would put it: "Writing is prayer."

From 1908 onward a few of Kafka's short pieces began appearing in a new Prague literary magazine called *Hyperion*, which was run by two of Brod's friends. Brod did his utmost to publicize Kafka's works, at one point reading out several pieces to Franz Werfel, who was at the time struggling to establish himself as a poet. Werfel laconically remarked of Kafka's works: "They won't get any further than Bodenbach." This was a town on the German border, and Werfel meant that Kafka's work would prove of no interest to anyone outside the Czech provinces. Although this was intended as a damning remark, it was in fact highly perceptive as well. From the beginning, Kafka's work would always remain peculiarly atmospheric of the narrow provincial setting in which it was written. Even later, when he chose to set his work in "Amerika" or some distant colonial penal colony, its intrinsic atmosphere would usually be that of a claustrophobic, somehow menacing province of the decaying Austro-Hungarian Empire. For years this would condemn Kafka's

41

works to neglect; only later would it be recognized as his peculiar originality and strength.

Max Brod was by now a leading literary figure in Prague. Several books of his poems had been published in Germany, to some acclaim; and his Berlin publishers had great hopes for his next novel, which showed stylistic influences of the latest Italian futurism. Brod had also become music critic for the German-language Prague daily newspaper. Despite such precocious success, he was still finding it difficult to earn a living. Like Kafka, he was forced to keep up a daytime job, and in the mornings he worked at the post office. Their shared plight drew the two friends even closer, and during their all too brief holidays they took to traveling abroad together.

In September 1909, Franz and Max traveled to the northern Italian resort of Riva, on Lake Garda. As neither of them had seen an aircraft before, they took a side trip to the flying display at Bescia, forty miles down the road. Among the thousands who attended this spectacular modern event, Kafka was excited to see several European celebrities, including the French flyer Louis

Blériot (who just two months earlier had been the first to fly the English Channel), the operatic composer Puccini ("with a nose that could be called the nose of a drinker," according to Kafka), and the flamboyant Italian poet Gabriele d'Annunzio ("dancing attendance on the Conte Oldofredi"). Brod encouraged Kafka to write up his diary notes of this occasion. The result was later shown by Brod to a Prague newspaper editor, who published a shortened version entitled "The Aeroplanes at Brescia."

Just over a year later the two friends traveled by way of Nuremberg to Paris. Kafka was not an easy traveling companion. In Paris he suffered from depression and took to disappearing on long solitary walks in order to spare the bewildered Brod his cheerless company. He then suffered an outbreak of boils, and returned alone to Prague. After visiting a doctor, he wrote back to Brod, obliquely hinting at a psychosomatic reason for his boils: "My idea, which I naturally didn't confide to the doctor, was that the pavements of Prague, Nuremberg, and above all Paris caused the eruption."

The following year Kafka and Brod jour-
neyed together to Leipzig, at the time the
publishing capital of Germany. When Brod exas-
peratedly closed the window of their room at
4 a.m. to keep out the racket of the passing de-
livery horses and market carts, and the rattle of
the early trams, Kafka lay in the dark feeling as
if he were "buried alive." Later Brod showed
some of Kafka's work to a publisher and intro-
duced him to Kafka. The publisher expressed an
interest in bringing out a book of Kafka's short
pieces. Later Kafka and Brod went to Weimar.
Here they visited Goethe's house, and over the
next few days Kafka developed an infatuation
for the curator's daughter. "Finally, on the way
home, definite contact without any real commu-
nication," he noted in his diary.

Around this time Brod took Kafka to see the
visiting Yiddish Theatre in Prague. It turned out
to be a significant event in Kafka's life, introduc-
ing him to his Jewish roots. He had only been
used to his father's constant mockery of "back-
ward" Jewish ways. Now he became passion-
ately interested in the Yiddish Theatre, and

perhaps inevitably became infatuated with its leading lady.

Kafka was now earning a reasonable salary and was able to develop his writing in his free time. But he felt unable to break away from his family and continued to live at home. As a result, the conflict with his overbearing "commonsensical" father—both in its real and its imagined aspects—continued as ever. Kafka's writing was regarded as a useless waste of time by his father, who viewed it in many ways as an affront to his philistine dignity. As Kafka observed, in a comment fraught with misunderstading: "My father only gets annoyed when he sees me at my desk late at night, because he thinks I work too hard." For his part, Kafka longed more than anything for his father to accept the one thing he knew his father found completely unacceptable—his writing. This struggle reached a head when Kafka's oldest sister Eli married Karl Hermann, who decided to use his dowry to set up a factory, the Prague Asbestos Works. Kafka's father saw this as the founding of a family industrial dynasty and would later come to see it as the ideal opportunity to turn his hapless son into a successful businessman. The factory was set up in the eastern suburb of Zizkov, with twenty-five workers and fourteen machines. Karl Hermann had to spend most of his time in the field, working as a solo sales force, leaving the factory in the charge of a foreman. Neither Karl nor Kafka's father trusted the foreman, and became convinced that whenever he was left on his own he was fiddling the books and allowing his workers to idle. In order to avert ruin, Kafka's father decided that his son Franz would look after the factory on such occasions. Characteristically, Kafka allowed himself to be browbeaten into this task.

It is difficult to imagine a man less suited to running a factory than the hypersensitive Kafka:

> Yesterday in the factory. The girls in their unbearably dirty and untidy clothes, their hair disheveled as though they had just got up, the expressions on their faces fixed by the incessant noise of the transmission belts and by the individual machines, automatic ones, of course, but unpredictably breaking

down. . . . When six o'clock comes and they
. . . untie the kerchiefs from around their
throats and their hair . . . you move back
against the greasy crates to make room for
them, hold your hat in your hand when they
say good evening, and do not know how to
behave when one of them holds your winter
coat for you to put on.

Early in the following year it was clear that the
factory was losing money, and Karl began insisting that Kafka's father increase his investment.
Hermann was furious and began blaming his
son. As Kafka noted in his diary: "Day before
yesterday, reproaches on account of the factory.
For an hour after that I lay on the couch and
thought about jumping out of the window."

When he saw Max Brod, he would pour out
his troubles. On one occasion, as they were walking through the streets of Prague, Kafka became
so immersed in his catalog of woes that he inadvertently stepped in front of an oncoming coach
and was all but run down. This produced a typically Kafkaesque reaction. "At that moment I

was actually furious at not being run over." He was so upset, in fact, that he stamped his foot in anger and appeared to curse. On seeing this, the coach driver swore at him, unaware that Kafka was purely angry at himself for not having put an end to his life.

Kafka's depressions deepened still further. As he wrote to the ever-faithful Max: "I stood for a long time at the window and pressed myself against the pane, and in many ways it would have suited me to [jump]. It also seems that survival causes less of an interruption to my writing than death." By now Brod was becoming alarmed and felt that the possibility of Kafka committing suicide was very real. He decided to act as best he could. Early in October 1911 he wrote a letter to Kafka's mother, enclosing the letter that Kafka had written to him about jumping out the window. Kafka's mother was suitably shocked, but even in this extreme situation she felt the need to avoid upsetting her husband. Instead she quietly told Franz to stop going to the factory. She then privately contacted her brother-in-law's brother and hired him to cover for her son. Meanwhile her husband was led to believe that Kafka was still conscientiously looking after things at the factory.

The effect on Kafka was little short of miraculous. Freed from his suicidal depression, he launched into writing a full-length novel called *Amerika* (originally entitled *The Missing Person*). Most of this was completed in October and November 1911. At the same time he also completed the short story that many regard as his most characteristic work, "Metamorphosis."

As Kafka wrote, when he had started into *Amerika*, "After 15 years of despairing effort (except for rare moments), this is the first major work in which, for the past 6 weeks, I have felt confidence." This sudden rush of rare confidence has an unsettling effect on the character of the novel's hero, the sixteen-year-old Karl Rossman. In many respects, Karl is a reflection of Kafka himself, exhibiting his blend of weakness and persistence. Yet the new positive component would make its anomalous appearance in Karl's moments of innocent optimism and flashes of resentment at his situation.

The book opens with Karl Rossman arriving on an ocean liner in New York harbor. He has been hurriedly dispatched to America after having been seduced by a thirty-five-year-old maid-servant who as a result has become pregnant. This has echoes of Kafka's first sexual experience, which took place during the hot summer of 1903 when he was a twenty-year-old student studying for his exams. Looking out the window he had noticed a shopgirl standing in a window opposite, and caught her eye. They had arranged to meet, and he had found her to be "a good-hearted friendly girl." Later they had gone together to a hotel on the far side of the river. Kafka's reactions to what happened had been characteristically ambivalent, this time with distinct neurotic undertones.

It was all, before the hotel, charming, exciting and vile; in the hotel it was no different. And when, towards morning, we went home over the Karlsbrücke [the famous bridge across the river in central Prague], it was still hot and beautiful, and I was certainly happy, but this happiness consisted only in my finally having peace from the constant whining of the body, but above all the happiness consisted in the whole thing's not being still more vile, still more filthy.

Despite such feelings, he went out with the girl again but was rescued from any deeper involvement when he had to accompany his parents on holiday. Kafka's memory of this incident is of interest for its revelation of his thought processes: his obstinate refusal to let himself be overwhelmed by any positive feelings, and the irresistible ambivalence that results from his self-knowledge. This is the "mature" Kafka, even if such maturity sits uneasily beside such neurosis. But in *Amerika*, Kafka has not yet learned how to assimilate such neurosis into profound ambivalence. Karl Rossman's experience with the maidservant Johanna is almost entirely grotesque:

She lay down next to him . . . pressed her naked stomach against his body, groped with her hand between his legs so disgustingly that

Karl shook his head and neck free of the pillows, then thrust her stomach several times against him, as though, it seemed, she were a part of him, and perhaps this was why he was seized terribly by the feeling of needing help. Weeping, he finally arrived in his own bed after she had several times asked him to come to her room again.

As Kafka worked through the night on *Amerika*, rereading this passage would affect him deeply—to such an extent that "I was nervous of waking my parents in the adjoining room with my uncontrollable sobbing." Although Kafka may have dismissed Freud's psychoanalysis as "a helpless error," there is no mistaking a deeply Freudian element in Kafka's behavior here.

From the outset, the America of Kafka's *Amerika* remains very much a figment of Kafka's imagination. As Karl Rossman "stood on the liner slowly entering the harbor of New York, a sudden burst of sunshine seemed to illuminate the Statue of Liberty, so that . . . the arm with the sword rose up as if newly stretched aloft." The transformation of the statue holding a torch into one holding a sword is emblematic of Kafka's "Amerika," which is seen as a corrupt, fairy-tale land, very much an Austro-Hungarian version of reality. This contributes to both the strength and the weakness of Kafka's novel.

The opening chapter, "The Stoker," is masterful Kafka, filled with subtle innuendo and menace, along with its incongruous elements of naiveté. As Karl Rossman prepares to disembark from the liner, he realizes that he has "forgotten his umbrella down below." When he proceeds to the lower decks, he gets lost "down endlessly recurring stairs, through corridors with countless turnings, through an empty room with a deserted writing table." Eventually he finds himself in the crew's quarters and bangs on a cabin door.

> "It isn't locked," a voice shouted from inside, and Karl opened the door with genuine relief. "What are you hammering at the door for, like a madman?" asked a huge man, scarcely even glancing at Karl. Through an opening of some kind a feeble glimmer of daylight, all

that was left after the top decks had used it up, fell into the wretched cubbyhole in which a bunk, a cupboard, a chair, and the man were packed together, as if they had been stored there.

This is his introduction to the stoker, who is also German like Karl. He and the stoker fall into conversation and end up lying on his bunk together. Karl learns that the stoker has a number of obscure grievances against the Romanian chief engineer Schubal, and decides to support the stoker by arguing his case before the captain. This meeting with the captain, his chief purser, the chief engineer, and the hapless stoker is interrupted by the arrival of Karl's Uncle Jacob, an American senator, who has come on board to fetch Karl. When the senator tries to lead his nephew away, Karl demands:

"What will happen to the stoker now?" "The stoker will get what he deserves," said the Senator, "and what the Captain considers to be right. I think we have had enough, and more than enough of the stoker, a view in which every gentleman here will certainly concur."

"But that's not the point in a question of justice," said Karl.

Karl eventually leaves the stoker to his fate. He goes to stay with his Uncle Jacob, and there begins his new life in America. This eventually develops into a series of quasi-picaresque adventures, which unfold in chapters with such titles as "A Country House Near New York," "The Road to Ramases," "The Hotel Occidental," and "A Refuge." Perhaps inevitably, this being a work by Kafka, the hero makes a mess of his life in the Austro-Hungarian version of the New World. His job and his relationships with those he meets end in shame, until eventually we come to the last chapter, entitled "The Nature Theatre of Oklahoma." This takes on a distinctly allegorical aspect, which nonetheless includes several amusing touches. The Nature Theatre is looking for new recruits, who are told to report to a nearby racetrack. Here the proceedings are intended as a parody of the Last Judgment. New recruits are signed on at the bookmakers' booths, with the names of the successful applicants appearing on the mechanical board that announces the winners. The novel ends with Karl boarding the train for Oklahoma, and our last view of him is traveling across the mountains.

"The Stoker" and "The Nature Theatre of Oklahoma" are the two most successful chapters in *Amerika*, but the trouble is they are completely different in manner, style, and even intention. *Amerika* has a certain unevenness throughout, but there is no mistaking the emergence, between the wobbles, of a distinctly original voice of considerable imaginative power. In 1911 in Europe, no one else was writing quite like this.

This is even more the case with the story that Kafka wrote at about the same time, "Metamorphosis." But here there are no wobbles: this is an astonishingly original masterpiece from a young writer who here finds his true voice. Like Karl Rossman in *Amerika*, the central character Gregor Samsa has a curiously inhuman flaw. He seems unable to register surprise at the predicament in which he finds himself. Indeed, he seems to accept his condition almost without question. His questioning is directed at how to redeem the situation. In *Amerika* this characteristic flaw became something of a literary flaw, unsettling our belief in Karl. In "Metamorphosis" it serves to render the hero's situation utterly and terrifyingly plausible. It is the acceptance of horror.

Gregor Samsa has become a large insect, and from the opening sentence you share his predicament. It is as if all that is weird in the human predicament has solidified into the terror and humiliation of his existence as a beetle. As with Kafka's *America*, there are also certain factual errors. For instance, early on in the story Gregor attempts to turn his cumbersome insect body on its side:

> However violently he forced himself towards his right side, he always rolled onto his back again. He tried it at least a hundred times, shutting his eyes to keep from seeing his struggling legs, and only desisted when he began to feel in his side a faint dull ache he had never experienced before.

Entomological critics have been quick to point out that insects have no eyelids and therefore cannot shut their eyes. Nabokov even argues that Samsa has become "a beetle with human eyes," and that this, together with the fact that "he still clings to human memories, human experience," means that "The metamorphosis is not quite complete as yet." This insight more than makes up for any antic pedantry on Nabokov's behalf. (He extends his entomological investigation of Gregor's condition by arguing that his "numerous little legs" cannot in fact be more than six or he "would not be an insect from a zoological point of view.") The entire point of Gregor's metamorphosis is that it is not complete. If it were, he would think and feel like an insect; he would be deprived of his crushing self-consciousness, and there would be nothing wrong with him. Instead he is visibly and painfully aware of his predicament as an insect-person. Externally he is completely transformed into an insect (regardless of his eyes), yet internally he remains very much a human being. There is, however, evidence that the metamorphosis has begun to take place internally as well—when Gregor, after trying vainly to turn on his side, becomes aware of "a faint dull ache he had never experienced before."

Gregor's insect appearance may be seen as simply a reification of his self-loathing. Symbolically, it is how Gregor has come to see his appearance in the eyes of others. Kafka has masterfully taken his own predicament that one step further—through the looking glass, so to speak. "Metamorphosis" is told in the third person, giving this most autobiographical of fantasies a grounded objectivity. It enables us to empathize with Gregor and understand his feelings as well as the feelings of those around him in the claustrophobic apartment in which the action unfolds.

Much of Kafka's fable-story is taken up with the family's reaction to the predicament of their son, and the effect this has on their home. Gregor had provided the main financial support for the family, allowing his father to retire and his sister Grete to take up violin lessons. But now they are left without support, forcing his father back to work.

Gregor's beloved sister Grete is initially sympathetic to his plight, making sure that he has suitable food. Despite this, she remains perturbed by his appearance. Even after a month, when she comes into his room early one morning and sees him gazing out of the window "not only did she retreat, she jumped back as if in alarm and banged the door shut." By now Gregor has begun to explore his new state, crawling over the furniture, walking up the walls and along the ceiling. "He especially liked to hang suspended from the ceiling; he could breathe easier; his body swayed lightly from side to side; and in the blissful state induced by hanging there it sometimes happened to his surprise that he let go and fell to the floor."

Grete decides that they should remove the furniture from Gregor's room, in order to allow him more freedom to move about. Yet his mother wants to leave the room as it is, so that "when he comes back to us [he] will find everything unchanged." Grete prevails; but when she and her mother are removing the furniture, Gregor suddenly dashes from his hiding place and runs up the wall to cover his favorite picture that he does not want them to remove. The sight of this "huge brown mass on the flowered wallpaper" causes his mother to faint, and in the confusion Gregor follows his sister out through the open door of his room.

When Mr. Samsa returns from work, Grete tells him that Gregor has escaped from his room. Gregor's father attempts to drive the insect back into his room by pelting him with small red apples. "An apple thrown without much force grazed Gregor's back and glanced off harmlessly. But another following immediately landed right on his back and sank in." This brought about a change:

The serious injury to Gregor, which disabled him for more than a month—the apple went on sticking in his body as a visible reminder since no one ventured to remove it—seemed to have made even his father recollect that Gregor was a member of the family, despite his present unfortunate and repulsive shape, and ought not to be treated as an enemy, that, on the contrary, family duty required the suppression of disgust and the exercise of patience, nothing but patience.

But Gregor's state now begins to deteriorate. The apple festers in his back, and he becomes, "covered in dust; hair and bits of old food stuck to his back and sides, and trailed after him." Grete no longer cleans his room.

In order to survive, the Samsa family is forced to take in lodgers, and three bearded clerks come to live in the crowded flat. One night when Grete begins playing her violin, the lodgers ask her to play for them. Gregor is attracted by the music and crawls into the room. "Was he really an animal if music could move him so?" he wonders to himself. Then one of the lodgers catches sight of Gregor; and is so disgusted and outraged that he gives notice: "In view of the revolting conditions prevailing in this house, I intend to quit my room immediately." The other two lodgers follow suit.

Now Grete decides that they must get rid of "the creature." Even Gregor himself is inclined to agree:

The decision that he must disappear was one that he held to even more strongly than his sister—if that were possible. In this state of vacant and peaceful meditation he remained until the clock tower struck three in the morning. The first broadening of light in the world outside the window entered his consciousness once more. Then his head sank to the floor of its own accord and from his nostrils came the last faint flicker of his breath.

By now the Samsa family have been forced to get rid of their servant girl and employ "a gigantic bony charwoman with white hair flying round her head." She has quickly developed the habit of poking her head around the door to Gregor's room and calling to him in an apparently friendly manner, "Come along, then, you old dung beetle!"

But this morning when she arrives, she notices him "lying motionless on purpose, pretending to be in the sulks; she credited him with every kind of intelligence." She pokes him with a broom and discovers that he is dead. At once she calls the Samsa family, who come in to view the corpse. When they emerge from Gregor's room, "They all looked a little as though they had been crying; from time to time Grete hid her face in father's arm."

The story ends by leaving the enclosed atmosphere of the apartment. After Gregor's death, the Samsa family decides to take a tram ride into the countryside. They appear relieved and wish to "Let bygones be bygones." On the journey, Mr. and Mrs. Samsa notice that their daughter "had bloomed into a pretty girl with a good figure . . . it would soon be time to find a good husband for her."

In August 1912, Kafka went to a party given by Max Brod, where he met a woman called Felice Bauer, an executive in a Berlin manufacturing firm—a rare position for a woman of the period, bespeaking an unusual degree of independence. She was twenty-five years old, four years younger than Kafka, though indicatively she thought that Kafka looked younger than her. In Kafka's words, she had a "bony, empty face that carried its emptiness openly. . . . Almost broken nose, blond, rather stiff, unappealing hair, strong chin." Later he sat down beside her and "I looked at her more carefully for the first time; as I was sitting there I'd already arrived at an irreversible judgement." This would be the woman in Kafka's life, to whom, over the next five years, he would write more than a thousand letters and postcards, on occasion posting up to three long letters a day.

It did not take long for Kafka to decide that he wanted to marry Felice, to surrender himself to her and live a normal life. Yet something in him was deeply averse to such ideas. He was certainly beset by sexual uncertainties. He longed for her yet needed to place her on a pedestal, whereupon the idea of sex with her became repulsive. (All this was present from the outset, as can be seen from his initial reactions to her at the party.) He was also aware that Felice was far from being convinced that she wanted to marry him, yet he insisted on being "fair" to her by describing to her his bad qualities. The result was a frenzy of confession and self-analysis from Kafka, all poured into letters with the appearance of extreme and meticulous self-knowledge.

Yet perhaps the most important thing about Kafka's relationship with Felice was that she lived in Berlin. Had she lived in Prague, he would never have committed himself to say what he did. At a distance, and in writing, his neuroses regarding relationships with women and marriage could be given full vent. Basically he saw the central problem of his relationship with Felice as a choice between marriage (normality, children, as well as escape from his father) and his writing (which was in many ways his only real life, the only place he could "pray," the only place he could breathe and attempt to come to terms with his existence). This dichotomy drove him to ecstasies of confession, paroxysms of self-analysis . . . and epistolatory logorrhea. Here he could confess his every uncertainty:

> . . . have you ever known uncertainty? Have you observed how, within yourself and independent of other people, diverse possibilities

open up in several directions, thereby actually creating a ban on your every movement?
Have you ever, without giving the slightest
thought to anyone else, been in despair simply about yourself?

By now Kafka was also keeping a diary, in which
he would record everyday events in his life, visits
to the café, the theatre, meetings with Brod, and
so forth. He also sketched scenes for unwritten
books and, most interestingly of all, similarly
written scenes from his own life. In one hilarious
passage he describes his attempt to have a black
dress suit made for him so that he can attend
dancing classes. A tailor is called to the house, but
Kafka does not want the sort of suit the tailor sug-
gests, and proposes a different suit. The tailor, for
his part, claims never to have heard of a suit such
as the one Kafka describes. But Kafka has seen
just such a suit in the window of a secondhand
shop on the other side of the Old Town Square,
and insists upon dragging the obstinate tailor
across the square to see it. Though when they arrive the suit is no longer in the window. . . . And

so it goes on. (This sequence is set down at length in From Kafka's Writings on pages 104–105.)

In his diaries Kafka was honing a subtle talent for expressing his existential bewilderment in a deadpan, often absurdist manner. His letters to Felice, on the other hand, enabled him to pour out his neurotic obsessions. In his letters he could indulge his obsessive self-analysis, leaving him free in his diaries to express his objective self-awareness. These two talents had coalesced in "Metamorphosis," but had remained concerned with the world of family. His next work would transcend this intense but limited milieu, extending his talent in both directions—so that his theme was both deeply subjective (in an objective manner) and universal (in an unmistakably Kafkaesque manner). Indeed, the adjective *Kafkaesque* finds its most profound and characteristic meaning in the novel that Kafka now began writing. This was to be called *The Trial*.

Its opening words lead us directly into the maze from which its central character strives throughout the novel to emerge: "Someone must have been telling lies about Joseph K., for without having done anything wrong he was arrested one fine morning. . . ." The words are both objective and chilling, and we realize at once that we are entering a menacing, nightmarish world. Yet according to Max Brod, when Kafka read out the opening pages of *The Trial* to him and a few friends, Kafka quickly had his audience reduced to stitches of laughter. Just as Kafka found himself plagued with angst in the midst of his comical attempt to have a dress suit made for him, he was also aware of the absurdity of a man being arrested for a crime he did not commit, and the subsequent failure of his endless attempts to get to the bottom of the matter. In concentrating on the darker side of our predicament we should never forget its absurdity, and absurdity's most immediate response is laughter. With this in mind, it is possible to look back at *Amerika*, or even "Metamorphosis," and see that they are both pervaded by an element of deep humor which is often overlooked. The staging of the Last Judgment as a day at the races can easily be seen as satirical farce, and with only a little more breadth of vision the plight of a human being transformed into a giant beetle can be recognized as the stuff of pantomime. It is always worth remembering that when Kafka himself read his works, he played them for laughs. The seamless objectivity of his fables and allegorical adventures allows for a great breadth of reaction. And it is this breadth which allows for a plethora of interpretation. A human-insect can be seen as ridiculous, tragic, farcical, a psychological parable, a philosophical fable . . . one reads in whatever one needs to take out. Here Kafka, in revealing himself, lets us reveal ourselves—hopefully to ourselves as well as to others. Any interpretation of Kafka involves self-revelation. Kafka laughed, and perhaps had to laugh to protect himself, to play it as a game. Yet it also becomes clear that Kafka is laughing at us, playing with us: what is it we see reflected in the mirror of his works?

The Trial is told in transparent, almost matter-of-fact language, though as we read on we become increasingly aware of more abstract and allegorical importance. The literal landscape of the story begins to grow deepening symbolic shadows which increasingly dominate the scene. Although it contains people, the spiritual atmosphere of *The Trial* is reminiscent of the canvases of Kafka's contemporary, Giorgio de Chirico, the Greek-Italian painter of desolate "metaphysical" urbanscapes. Kafka's novel relates the story of Joseph K.'s search to determine why he has been arrested, and increasingly turns into a young man's struggle against the elusive but threatening powers that determine his fate.

The two officials who come to Joseph K.'s apartment to arrest him claim that they are "not authorized" to tell him why he is being arrested. "Proceedings against you have begun, and you will be told everything in due course." But this is precisely what does not happen. Throughout the novel, K. goes from place to place in the attempt to discover the nature of his alleged crime and why he is being charged. (After the opening, Joseph K. quickly becomes plain K., for the most part. Kafka appeared to feel at ease with this more objective yet more identifying cipher.) In the course of K.'s quest, he discovers that "there are court offices in almost every attic." Hidden behind the façade of the everyday world, it seems there is "a summary court in perpetual session." He has discussions about his situation with his landlady, who regards his case as "something learned which I don't understand." When he protests to the offical that he has no knowledge of any law that he appears to have broken, the official replies that he will soon "get the feel of it." Later on, he also discusses matters with the painter Tintorelli, who informs him that there are vast numbers of judges, and that once he has been charged, his case can never be dropped. Tintorelli tells the bewildered K., "If I were to paint all the judges in a row on one canvas and you were to plead your case before it, you would have more hope of success than before the actual court." As ever, Tintorelli's statements are open to many interpretations. Kafka may be suggesting here that intercession through art could well bring more "success" than any "actual" way of attempting to understand the nature of our predicament.

At one point K. encounters a priest in the cathedral. The priest initially addresses K. from the pulpit, as if delivering a sermon. But later he steps down, telling K., "I had to speak to you first from a distance. Otherwise I am too easily influenced and tend to forget my duty."

K. is encouraged, and tells the priest, "You are an exception amongst those who belong to the Court. I have more trust in you than in any of the others, though I know many of them. With you I can speak openly."

"Don't be deluded," says the priest, and proceeds to tell K. a story, which is cast in the form of a parable and seems to hold the key to what is going on. This parable is sometimes entitled "Before the Law," and originates from "writings which preface the Law,"—hinting at its quasi-biblical status.

In the story, a man approaches the door to the Law. This stands open, but the man is not permitted to enter by the doorkeeper, "in his furred robe, with his huge pointed nose and long, thin Tartar beard." The man learns that the doorkeeper is in fact just the first doorkeeper, and even if he managed to get through this door he would only encounter other doors guarded by ever more formidable doorkeepers who would prevent him from entering. This comes as a surprise to the man, who had always assumed that the Law was open to all. He decides to wait until he is granted permission to enter. The doorkeeper even brings him a stool to sit on. The man waits for days, which eventually stretch into years, but all to no avail. He even tries to bribe the doorkeeper, who accepts all his bribes with no qualms. The doorkeeper informs the man that he accepts the bribes just so that the man won't feel that he has left something untried. As the man waits, his attitude changes: "In the first years he curses his evil fate aloud; later, as he grows old, he only mutters to himself." As time goes by, "he has learned to know even the fleas in the doorkeeper's fur collar." Eventually he knows that he will soon die, so he beckons the doorkeeper and asks him why, in all the years he has been waiting, no one else has come to the door. The doorkeeper informs him that no one else could get in through this door, as it is intended solely for him. Then he closes the door.

Typically, Kafka now goes on to suggest various conflicting interpretations of this story. The priest's explanations are both enigmatic and simplistic. Kafka is suggesting that we should come to our own conclusions. As ever, we can see in his work what we need to see. The depth of our interpretation reflects the depths of our understanding. Or so he would have us believe. If we believe in some ultimate form of justice (metaphysical or otherwise), we may see our lack of access to this as part of our human condition. Or maybe there is no such thing as the Law, and any attempt to gain access to it is simply futile, a waste of our life. All we know for certain is that the man can never gain admittance to the Law.

Yet all this is much more than the discovery of some obscure objective destiny, however profoundly it may control the real world around us. Throughout much of the narrative K. remains peculiarly free. He is able to go about his business and live his personal life as well as pursue his inquiries regarding the Court and the nature of his case. Ultimately the full extent of K.'s powerlessness becomes clear to him. When he finally understands this, he offers no further resistance to his inevitable fate.

The ending of *The Trial* is particularly bleak. "On the evening before K.'s thirty-first birthday," two men come to his lodgings. "It was about nine o'clock, the time when a hush falls on the streets." The two men are dressed "in frock-coats, pallid and plump, with top-hats." K. is eventually led by the two men out of town, across some fields, to "a small, stone quarry, deserted and bleak." Here "the moon shone down on everything with that simplicity and serenity which no other light possesses." The two men take off their top hats, and after "an exchange of courteous formalities" they remove K.'s coat, waistcoat, and shirt, then lay him down on the ground. One of them now produces "a long, thin, double-edged butcher's knife." K. has by now realized that these are his executioners, and it becomes clear to him that they expect him to take the knife and do their job for them. But "he could not completely rise to the occasion, he could not relieve the officials of all their tasks; the responsibility for this last failure of his lay with him who had not left him the remnant of strength necessary for the deed." In a characteristic Kafkaesque touch, this final omission is not an act of defiance but one of weakness—seemingly physical but almost certainly psychological as well, its responsibility lying with the person who had deprived him of "the strength necessary for the deed." A few moments later he asks himself, "Were there some arguments in his favor that he had overlooked? Of course there must be. Logic is doubtless unshakable, but it cannot withstand a man who wants to go on living. Where was the Judge whom he had never seen? Where was the High Court to which he had never penetrated?" One of the executioners places his hands around K.'s throat while the other thrusts the knife into his heart and turns it twice. "With failing eyes K. could still see the two of them, cheek leaning against cheek, immediately before his face, watching the final act. 'Like a dog!' he said; it was as if he meant the shame of it to outlive him."

Throughout the course of the novel the allegorical and the personal are skillfully interwoven and remain present at all times. K.'s circumstances bear certain recognizable similarities to those of Franz Kafka, and the woman with whom he is obscurely involved is called Fraulein Bürstner, whose name in the original manuscript was abbreviated to the initials F. B., the same as those of Felice Bauer. Joseph K.'s feelings of guilt are both those of the author and those that are an integral part of our Western humanity. The origins of this guilt can be found in both "the Fall" of Judeo-Christianity and the repressions suggested by Freudian psychoanalysis—indeed, they appear to be part of our human condition in all its most profound aspects. Our Western psychology, our religion, much of our philosophy, even our sociology and aspects of our political impulse seem to involve the existence of guilt—involving repression or a fall from grace—and Kafka leaves room for one, several, or all of these interpretations in *The Trial*. His novel can just as easily be seen as describing the impossibility of its author coming to terms with the overwhelming presence of his father: life at home was a continuous "trial." It can also be seen as the fate of humanity, the fate of Jews in central European society, even the fate of all citizens of Austro-Hungary, living beneath the all-pervasive, ramshackle bureaucracy of a decaying empire.

This political aspect has led many to see *The Trial* as a work of prophecy, presaging events that would occur in the decades following Kafka's death: Joseph K.'s fate would be the fate of the Jews in Hitler's fascist Europe—here were the first inklings of the Holocaust. Others, under Communist tyranny, recognized their own fate in that of Joseph K. As the persecuted Russian poet Anna Akhmatova declared when she first read Kafka's work during the Stalinist era, "He was writing about us."

Such prophetic readings are difficult to defend on rational grounds, compelling though they may be. They are more a credit to Kafka's skill in leaving his work open to a breadth of interpretation. There is not a shred of evidence, in all of Kafka's voluminous writings, that he in any way foresaw the historical events that would unfold in the mid-twentieth century. On the other hand, his hypersensitivity—and his ability to universalize this in such works as *The Trial*—make it legitimate to read large-scale horrors into what for him were purely personal ones. What Akhmatova recognized was what Kafka felt, not the other way around, uncannily similar though these feelings may have been.

Soon after Kafka began writing *The Trial*, Europe was plunged into the First World War. Many of Kafka's friends were called up in the general mobilization that swept the Austro-Hungarian Empire, though he himself was exempt from conscription. His status as a quasi-government official, his poor health, and the fact that Jews were mostly rejected for military service, all ensured that he remained a noncombatant—thus contributing another source of guilt. Throughout the period of the war, Kafka's diaries remain as self-preoccupied as ever, but we know from Brod that Kafka did not remain aloof to what was going on around him. These events in the real world, and particularly the collapse of the Austro-Hungarian Empire which followed the war, certainly colored Kafka's work, though in the oblique fashion so typical of their author.

While he was writing *The Trial*, Kafka at last managed to move out of his family home, at least temporarily. He was now thirty-one and earning quite enough to support himself independently, but his ties to his family (especially his father) remained as complex as ever. He appeared to need this affliction. And despite devoting so much of his energy to writing *The Trial*, he continued his voluminous correspondence with Felice Bauer, pouring out his fears, his hopes, his angst, and even his love. It is possible to see this as the psychical material that he did not transform into the consummate art of *The Trial*—yet once again he seemed to need this bleeding sore of affliction. His unsparing self-analysis would later lead him to conclude: "Letter writing is an intercourse with ghosts, not only with the ghost of the receiver, but with one's own, which emerges between the lines of the letter."

During his entire five-year "correspondence-relationship" with Felice Bauer, Kafka actually met her for only a few weeks, and most of this time proved fraught enough to provide material for dozens of further letters attempting to explain every nuance of misunderstanding that had taken place. They became engaged twice, and disengaged twice. On one occasion they went on holiday together, and in Kafka's words they succumbed to "the disease of the instincts" on this occasion—hardly an attitude on which to found a marriage. Again and again their relationship approached a breaking point, but Kafka could not bring himself finally to call it off. By the end he was having nightmares in which "I shouted endlessly all along the streets, while again and again she grabbed at me, again and again the siren's clawed hands struck sideways or over my shoulders at my breast." Once again Kafka's words appear uncannily prescient. By now his hypochondria was beginning to give way to more realistic ailments. He had begun spitting blood. Then he suffered a hemorrhage of the lungs, and tuberculosis was diagnosed. It was more than a dream hand that had "clawed . . . at his breast"; he now had an irreproachable reason for telling Felice that marriage was out of the question, and they broke up for the last time.

But his illness did not deter Kafka from embarking upon other affairs, one of which was with the young Czech writer Milena Jesenska-Polak. A few limited editions of Kafka's stories had now begun to appear in German, and Milena wrote to Kafka asking for permission to translate some of these into Czech. Milena was an independent woman who was separated from her husband and lived in Vienna. Kafka was soon involved in another intense correspondence, alternating his charming and his confessional self, drawing them both into increasing intimacy. Eventually, after some coaxing from Milena, they met in Vienna. The forthright Milena managed to calm Kafka's fears. They walked in the woods together and took picnics; Kafka's hypochondria, and even his telltale cough, appear to have vanished in the summer sunshine. They were in love, and they made love, like happy lovers: Kafka even admitted to happiness: "fragments . . . torn from the night." Then he returned to Prague. In the midst of their increasingly hectic, confessional correspondence,

Milena decided that she could not leave her husband. Still, they continued to correspond, almost as intensely as before, and Milena continued to take an interest in Kafka's work. She, more than any other woman, perhaps more than any human being except Brod, understood Kafka the man and his work. "He saw a world of invisible demons that make war on helpless human beings and destroy them."

At about this time Kafka published one of his most compelling and resonant short stories, "In the Penal Colony." Here, more than ever before, Kafka succeeds in uniting the personal and the seemingly prophetic in a parable of horrific reality. An explorer visits a penal settlement on a tropical island, where he is asked to witness the execution of a prisoner. In many ways the story is a mirror image of *The Trial*, which Kafka was writing at the same time. In this case the prisoner has no idea of his crime, has had no opportunity to defend himself, and does not even know that he has been sentenced. Like Joseph K., he too is compared to a dog: being said to look like "a submissive little dog." But the story is not told

84

from his point of view; instead it is related from the point of view of the explorer, who has unwittingly, and unwillingly, become involved in the proceedings.

The officer in charge of the execution is particularly proud of the elaborate machine that is used to put the condemned to death, and he demonstrates how it works. The prisoner is strapped face down onto a bed, and a vibrating harrow made of glass needles then descends on him, slowly digging its needles deeper into the skin. These are adjusted so that they actually etch the words of the prisoner's unknown sentence into his back. The officer proudly explains:

> There are two kinds of needles. . . . The long needle does the writing, and the short needle sprays a jet of water to wash away the blood and keep the inscription clear. . . . Of course the script can't be a simple one; it's not supposed to kill a man straight off, but only after an interval of, on average, twelve hours; the turning point is reckoned to come at the sixth hour. . . . Enlightenment comes to the

most dull-witted. . . . You have seen how difficult it is to decipher the script with one's eyes; but our man deciphers it with his wounds.

The harrow eventually pierces his entire body, and then the machine efficiently tips him into the grave alongside.

In a characteristic twist, the officer notices the explorer's disapproval and sets the condemned man free. Instead he decides to demonstrate the machine on himself. He allows himself to be strapped to the bed, and the machine is turned on. But instead of functioning smoothly and etching its message into his back, the machine begins to disintegrate and grotesquely mangles the body of the officer.

Despite the sado-masochistic elements of "In the Penal Colony," which certainly echo an aspect of Kafka's psychology, the form and power of the work transcends such purely personal interpretations. This is a parable of power and control: here is the raw effect of the Law, in all its crudity. From the outset, the efficient rationale behind the execution is undermined by the sheer squalor of the actual proceedings. The fastidious Kafka spares the reader none of the blood and vomit involved. There is an almost visceral feeling of filth, which cannot be cleansed:

> When the officer had at length finished his task, he . . . went over to wash his hands in the water-bucket, perceived too late that it was disgustingly dirty, was unhappy because he could not wash his hands, in the end thrust them into the sand—this alternative did not please him, but he had to put up with it. . . .

The officer, who believes utterly in the system with its smooth-running mechanism and sophisticated effects, is the one who is devoured by it most gruesomely. In the end his devotion demonstrates nothing but the machine's brutality. There is no message etched on his back for his enlightenment; he is merely stabbed and bludgeoned to death. The political metaphors are evident and subtly conveyed; their prescience is uncanny. The psychology of those who connived in and perpetrated the Holocaust and Stalin's Terror is laid bare. Kafka may not have foreseen that such things would take place, but he undeniably understood *how* such things take place. And all this came from the suffering endured, and generated, by one man in solitude.

Kafka was aware, and yet on occasion curiously unaware, of this. How else can one explain the fact that this was the very story he chose to present to his father in an attempt to justify himself, his writing, his very existence? When "In the Penal Colony" was published, Kafka offered a copy to his father—who offhandedly told him to "put it on the bedside table." These unfeeling words would remain etched forever on Kafka's sensibilities. This personal aspect of the story is also astonishingly prescient. He did not know when writing the story, or even when offering it, that his father would react so heartlessly, that the effect of this rejection would mark him for years to come. The latter fact is revealed in a long letter that Kafka later addressed to his father. This is an intense psychological document of heartrending candor. Its unsparing self-analysis lays bare his labyrinthine relationship, real and imagined, with his father, even to the extent of finally confessing, self-defeatingly, "life is more than a Chinese puzzle." The letter opens as it means to go on:

> Dear Father,
>
> You asked me recently why I maintain I am afraid of you. As usual, I was unable to think of any answer to your question, partly for the very reason that I am afraid of you, and partly because an explanation of the grounds for this fear would mean going into far more details than I could even approximately keep in mind while talking. And if I now try to give you an answer in writing, it will still be very incomplete. . . .

This "incomplete" version continues for more than twenty thousand words, and Kafka confesses that even then "the magnitude of the subject goes far beyond the scope of my memory and power of reasoning." (Kafka's father would never read this letter. Kafka gave it to his mother to give to him, but she decided that its contents would only upset him, and returned it to her son.)

Kafka evidently needed these forays into the muddy waters of depth psychology in order to clear the way for the objective but cunningly deceptive lucidity of his literary works. For it was now that he started into the second of his full-length masterpieces, *The Castle*. The opening words of the novel set the scene:

> It was late in the evening when K. arrived. The village was deep in snow. The Castle hill was hidden, veiled in mist and darkness, nor was there even a glimmer of light to show that a castle was there. On the wooden bridge leading from the main road to the village, K. stood for a long time gazing into the illusory emptiness above him.

The "illusory emptiness" which K. sees is but the first of many uncertainties in the novel. K. (this time a mere cipher from the outset) arrives in the village claiming that he is a land surveyor who has been appointed by the Castle authorities. But has a land surveyor been appointed by the Castle? The suspicion is planted that K. may never have been appointed at all to such a post, that he may in fact be impersonating a land surveyor appointed by the Castle. From the very beginning of the novel, K.'s status is in question. All he knows, and all we know, is that he requires some kind of official recognition from the Castle, a permit of sorts, if he is to be allowed to stay in the village. The central theme of the novel is K.'s persistent attempt to penetrate the Castle authorities so that he can obtain a permit, and the apparent thwarting of his attempts by these same elusive authorities. On the morning after his arrival, K. is disappointed by his first sight of the Castle standing above the village:

> It was neither an old fortress nor a new mansion, but a dismal collection of innumerable small buildings packed together. Swarms of crows circled around the only tower.

The novel has an oppressive atmosphere. It is deepest winter, the village is covered in snow, and most of the scenes take place after dark, usually in dim interiors.

Two assistants arrive to help K. in his work. They appear to have been sent by the Castle, yet K. also seems to have been expecting "my old assistants I told to follow me here." The two assistants, Arthur and Jeremiah, appear like two comic fools from the Yiddish Theatre, of which Kafka was so fond. They not only provide a certain clownish relief from the eerie menace of K.'s situation in the village, they also point up the comic vein that runs through the entire novel (one that might otherwise be overlooked). Here, as in *The Trial*, K.'s predicament is to a certain extent absurd. Besides being a deeply bewildered hero, his situation is also ridiculous. K. doesn't appear to recognize his "old assistants," who are not only late but have forgotten their apparatus, and on top of this they claim to know nothing about surveying. This floats the suggestion that they are not K.'s assistants, yet at the same time implies that K. is not a land surveyor summoned by the Castle authorities.

K. is obliged to move to another inn. Here he is informed by the landlord that the rooms "are reserved exclusively for gentlemen from the Castle." But it turns out that there is in fact only one

Castle official in residence, a man of some importance called Klamm. Even so, K. is informed that "he must not go anywhere except in the bar."

The novel has a strong erotic undercurrent throughout, with K. encountering a succession of more or less complaisant women. In the bar of the inn, K. encounters a young woman called Frieda, who is behind the counter serving beer. "As soon as her eye met K.'s it seemed to him that her look decided something about him." In pursuance of his quest to gain access to the Castle, K. asks Frieda if she knows Klamm. Freida offers to let K. peep through a hole in the door to Klamm's room.

> At a desk in the middle of the room sat Herr Klamm, his face brilliantly lit by an incandescent lamp which hung low before him. A middle-sized, plump, and ponderous man. His face was still smooth, but his cheeks were already somewhat flabby with age.

Klamm's very ordinariness somehow adds to the elusiveness and menace of his power, and the power of the Castle itself. (Kafka understood the banality of evil long before this phrase was coined.) K. is eventually left alone with Frieda and learns that she is Klamm's mistress. K. is given a place to sleep under the bar, but later Freida comes and lies down beside him. Frieda is presented as an independent, forthright character, and appears to have been based heavily upon Kafka's lover Milena. It is indicative that Frieda alone among the characters in the novel appears to penetrate the aura of isolation that surrounds K. Despite this, the author's deep ambivalence toward women and sexuality remain. Frieda and K. embrace, rolling together "among the beer slops and accumulated garbage on the floor." Yet at the same time K. "felt he was losing himself or wandering into a strange country, farther than man had ever wandered before, a country so strange that not even the air had anything in common with his native air." In this state, during which "hours went past," they eventually rolled against the door to Klamm's room. By now K.'s "enchantment was such that one could only go on and lose oneself further. So it came to him not as a shock but as a faint glimmer of comfort when from Klamm's room a deep, authoritative impersonal voice called for Frieda." A curious reaction indeed! Frieda vows to K. that she will never go to Klamm again, and defiantly bangs on his door, crying, "I'm with the land surveyor!"

Previously, the women in Kafka's novels have been little more than objects of the central character's desire. K. too had been little more than a passive entity in *The Trial*, bereft of wonder or indignation at what was happening to him. In *The Castle*, the central character takes on a more aggressive stance, especially in his attitude toward the officials who impede his way to the Castle. This has been seen as a reflection of Kafka's growing confidence in himself and his willingness to take charge of his life.

The twists and turns of K.'s ever-thwarted quest continue until the closing page of the novel, which ends abruptly after a scene that is in no way final. It looks as if Kafka could find no means of satisfactorily bringing the novel to a conclusion. Although this is unacceptable from an aesthetic, or purely literary, point of view, it does leave the novel open to a wider interpretation than might otherwise have been the case. We are left with the feeling that there is no possible final answer to such a quest. Indeed, our life, as long as we are living it, remains very much open-ended (if we accept the fact that death itself, the termination of our experience, is by its very nature beyond our experience). On the other hand, Max Brod claimed that it was Kafka's intention to end the novel with K., exhausted by his vain efforts to gain admittance to the Castle, lying on his deathbed. Just before he expires, he at last receives a permit from the Castle allowing him to live and work in the village.

The Castle has given rise to all manner of interpretations, from the profound to the ludicrous. The Castle is both K.'s ambition and the death of him (if we accept Brod's version). His relationship to it is both that of an imposter and that of a man constantly deceived. Once again K.'s situation is both highly personal (echoing Kafka's undermining uncertainties, his dealings with Milena and other women) and recognizably objective (in its alienation, its allegory of power, its metaphysical fable). As ever, Kafka leaves us free to derive our own meaning, arising from our own particular social, psychological, philosophical, or religious needs. He playfully hints at all such interpretations. How do we survey the world in which we live? Yet are we really surveyors at all? What right have we to make any claims as to our own status? Why do we feel the constant need to validate our existence?

By the time Kafka finished *The Castle* his tuberculosis had worsened. He had already been forced to take early retirement from the Workers' Accident Insurance Institute and was living on his pension. Between periods of writing, he spent intervals convalescing in various sanatoriums. After a protracted separation from Milena, in the summer of 1922 he finally broke free from his family, free from the claustrophobic atmosphere of Prague, and traveled to Berlin. Here he met an attractive nineteen-year-old Sephardic Jewess called Dora Dymant. She appears to have established an immediate rapport with Kafka, understanding both his temperament and his qualities. She later remembered: "Kafka had the bearing of a lonely man who's always in relation to something outside himself." By September 1922 they were sharing a small apartment in Berlin and learning Hebrew together. Kafka was aware that he probably did not have long to live, and before leaving Prague he had already instructed Brod to destroy all his literary works in the event of his death. He now regarded his move to Berlin as "the greatest achievement of my life." Even so, he continued writing. The two short stories he produced during this period—"The Burrow" and "Josephine the Singer"—are among his most poignant. But by now Germany was in the midst of the "hyperinflation crisis"; currency became virtually worthless, long queues had to be endured for even basic commodities, and hunger became rife in Berlin. Yet despite everything, it would appear that during this period Kafka came as near as he could to experiencing happiness. He had achieved what he thought was impossible: he was able to write and live with a woman at the same time. His relationship with Dora was direct and loving; there was no need for the endless analysis and self-laceration of his letter writing; they were together. They needed each other, and for the first time Kafka was able to accept such need.

This respite was to be short. Kafka's health soon worsened, and in March 1924 he was forced to return to Prague and live with his family. His great attempt to break free had ended in failure. By now his tuberculosis had spread from his lungs into his larynx, and he could barely speak. In April he traveled with Dora to Vienna, where he entered a sanatorium. Here he could only communicate by written notes. Despite being given morphine, the pain was now so great that Kafka wrote a note to his doctor: "Kill me or else you are a murderer." On June 3, less than two months after leaving Prague, Kafka died. His body was brought back to Prague, where Max Brod spoke at his funeral. This was briefly interrupted when Dora threw herself on Kafka's grave, weeping inconsolably.

Afterword

Kafka's body was buried in the New Jewish Cemetery in the eastern suburbs of Prague. The simple tombstone was inscribed with the name Dr. Franz Kafka. His parents evidently felt it appropriate only to mention his legal doctorate: no reference was made to the fact that he was a writer. In 1931 his father died and was buried beside him. Three years later his mother died and was also buried in the family plot. All three names were inscribed on the same tombstone. Even in death, Kafka did not escape his family or their lack of recognition of his achievement.

Yet in many ways these were the lucky ones. The New Jewish Cemetery was on land that had been purchased in the previous century by the Jewish community to relieve pressure on the burial plots in the Jewish quarter of the city. To ensure no recurrence of overcrowding, the community had purchased a large plot of land, considered sufficient for the foreseeable future. Even by the time the Kafka family were buried here, only a fraction of the cemetery had been filled. Today large tracts of the cemetery remain empty, and will never be filled. In 1938 the Nazis overran Czechoslovakia, and in the ensuing Holocaust the Middle European Jewish culture out of which Kafka had grown was destroyed. All three of Kafka's sisters, as well as countless cousins and other relatives, perished in the death camps. So did Milena, who was not Jewish; her outspoken socialist views sealed her fate. Felice Bauer, with whom Kafka had corresponded so incessantly, was married in Berlin and managed to flee to America, taking Kafka's letters with her. Dora Dymant also escaped, dying in London in 1952. Max Brod managed to reach Israel, where he supervised the publication and translation of Kafka's manuscripts, finally dying in Tel Aviv in 1968 at the age of eighty-four.

By then Kafka's works had been published in all major languages, and he was becoming recognized as one of the greatest writers of the twentieth century. His influence permeated far and wide, proving seminal in two other major writers of the century, the blind Argentinian Jorge Luis Borges and the exiled Irishman Beckett. In their isolation and personal mythmaking they would both, in their own separate ways, make Kafka their own.

Yet Kafka's influence was to transcend literature, permeating many spheres of intellectual life, each of which would react to him in its own characteristic way. Psychologists had a field day with Kafka's father fixation, many seeing this as the "explanation" of his entire life and works. Kafka's lucid and self-conscious revelations of his sex life provided further grist for the psychoanalytic mill. Kafka in Psycholand became a popular topic for analysts with literary aspirations, rivaling even such classic targets as Oedipus and Hamlet. And Kafka had a bonus here;

unlike these two classic literary fall guys, Kafka had actually existed!

In a similar vein, Kafka was also appropriated by the Surrealists, who welcomed him as a brother to their absurdist world. Kafka's effect on several Surrealist painters would prove of lasting worth. Likewise, fashionable post–Second World War existentialist philosophers also saw Kafka as one of their own. Ironically, Kafka was in many ways the ultimate anti-existentialist. His life can be seen as one long evasion of "authenticity," a simplistic notion of which he despaired; at the same time his works were deftly emptied of any explicit philosophical stance. Less savory twentieth-century "philosophies," such as fascism and communism, were quick to ban his works. He understood them, and the world they created, all too well: he had tyrannized himself, imposing upon himself a dictatorship from which he could never escape. His descriptions of his attempts to escape are his great works of art.

From Kafka's Writings

In this passage from Kafka's Diaries, *he discusses with a tailor a black dress suit that he wants made, so that he can attend dancing classes:*

. . . Since I regarded a tail coat as a fearful revolution one could forever talk about but on which one could never decide, we agreed on a tuxedo, which, because of its similarity to the usual sack coat, seemed to me at least bearable. But when I heard that the vest of the tuxedo had to be cut low and I would therefore have to wear a stiff shirt as well, my determination almost exceeded my strength, since something like this had to be averted. I did not want such a tuxedo, rather, if I had to have one . . . one that could be buttoned high. The tailor had never heard of such a tuxedo, but remarked that no matter what I intended to do with such a jacket, it couldn't be worn for dancing. Good, then it couldn't be worn for dancing, I didn't want to dance anyhow. . . . I wanted the jacket made for me as I had described it. The tailor's stubbornness was increased by the fact that until now I had always submitted with shamed haste to being measured for new clothes and to having them tried on, without expressing any opinions or wishes. So there was nothing else for me to do . . . but to go with him . . . across the Altstadter Ring [Old Town Square] to a secondhand clothing store in the window of which I had for quite some time seen displayed a simple tuxedo and had recognized it as suitable for me. But unfortunately it had already been removed from the window, I could not see it inside the store even by looking my hardest, I did not dare go into the store just to look at the tuxedo, so we returned, disagreeing as before. . . . I used my annoyance with the pros and cons of the argument as an excuse to send the tailor away with some small order or

KAFKA IN 90 MINUTES

other and an indefinite promise about the tuxedo while I . . . remained . . . barred forever . . . from girls, an elegant appearance, and dances. The instantaneous cheerfulness that this induced in me made me miserable, and besides, I was afraid that I had made myself ridiculous before the tailor as none of his customers had before.

A passage from the "Before the Law" section in The Trial, *where the old man has been sitting for years before the doorway to the Law:*

Now his life is drawing to a close. Before he dies, all that he has experienced during the whole time of his sojourn condenses in his mind to one question, which he has never yet put to the doorkeeper. He beckons the doorkeeper, since he can no longer raise his stiffening body. The doorkeeper has to bend far down to hear him, for the difference in size between them has increased very much to the man's disadvantage. "What do you want to know?" asks the doorkeeper; "you are insatiable." "Everyone strives to attain the Law," answers the man, "how does it come about, then, that in all these years no one has come seeking admittance but me?" The door-keeper perceives that the man is at the end of his strength and his hearing is failing, so he bellows in his ear: "No one but you could gain admittance through this door, since the door was intended only for you. I am now going to shut it."

This passage is taken from The Castle, *where K. meets his two assistants:*

He took the lantern from his host's hand and turned the light upon them; it was the men he had already met, who were called Arthur and Jeremiah. They now saluted him. That reminded him of his soldiering days, happy days for him, and he laughed. "Who are you?" he asked, looking from one to the other. "Your assisstants," they answered. "It's your assistants," corroborated the landlord in a low voice. "What?" said K., "are you my old assistants whom I told to follow me and whom I am expecting?" They answered in the affirmative. "That's good," observed K. after a short pause, "you've come very late, you're very slack." "It was a long way to come," said one of them. "A long way?" repeated K., "but I met you just now, coming from the Castle." "Yes," said they without further explanation. "Where is the apparatus?" asked K. "We haven't any," said they. "The apparatus I gave you?" said K. "We haven't any," they reiterated. "Oh, you are fine fellows!" said K., "do you know anything about surveying?" "No," said they. "But if you are my old assistants you must know something about it," said K. They made no reply. "Well, come in," said K., pushing them before him into the house.

This passage is taken from "Investigations of a Dog," in which the first-person narrator is a dog:

My questions only serve as a goad to myself; I only want to be stimulated by the silence which rises up around me as the ultimate answer. "How long will you be able to endure the fact that the world of dogs, as your researches make more and more evident, is pledged to silence and always will be? How long will you be able to endure it?" That is the real great question of my life, before which all smaller ones sink into insignificance; it is put to myself alone and concerns no one else. Unfortunately I can answer it more easily than the smaller, more specific questions. I shall very likely die in silence and surrounded by silence, indeed almost peacefully, and I look forward to that with composure. An admirably strong heart, lungs that it is impossible to use up before their time, have been given to us dogs as if in malice; we survive all questions, even our own, bulwarks of silence that we are.

A passage from Gustav Janouch's Conversations with Kafka, *showing that in his day-to-day life Kafka took a more than passing interest in current events, and indeed seems to have shown as much prescience here as in his literary works:*

I entered Kafka's office. There was nobody there. Papers lying open, two pears on a plate, a few newspapers were evidence that he was in the building. So I sat in the "visitors chair" near his writing table, picked up the *Prager Tagblatt*, and began to read.

After a little while Kafka came in.

"Have you been waiting long?"

"No, I have been reading." I showed him an article in the newspaper on the League Assembly.

Kafka made a helpless gesture.

"The League! Is it in any real sense a league of nations? It seems to me that the title League of Nations is only a disguise for a new battlefield."

"Do you mean that the League is not a peace organization?"

"The League is a machinery for localizing the battle. The war continues, only now with other weapons. Banks take the place of divisions; the fighting capacity of finance takes the place of the war potential of industry. The League is not a league of nations: it is a stock exchange for various groups of interest."

Some typical entries taken from Kafka's Diaries, *showing the range of his preoccupations as well as affording glimpses of his life and work:*

Desire for a deeper sleep that dissolves more. The metaphysical urge is only the urge toward death.

19 July [1912]. Rainy day. You lie in bed and the loud thrumming of the rain on the cabin roof is as if it were beating against one's own breast. Drops appear at the edge of the eaves as mechanically as a row of lights lit along a street. Then they fall. An old man suddenly charges across the meadow like a wild animal, taking a rain bath. The drumming of the drops in the night. As though one were sitting in a violin case. Running in the morning, the soft earth underfoot.

6 January [1915]. For the time being abandoned "Village Schoolmaster" and "The Assistant Attorney." But almost incapable too of going on with *The Trial*. Thinking of the girl from Lemberg. A promise of some kind of happiness resembles the hope of an eternal life. Seen from a distance it holds its ground, and one doesn't venture nearer.

111

I had agreed to go picnicking on Sunday with two friends, but quite unexpectedly slept past the hour when we were to meet. My friends, who knew how punctual I ordinarily am, were surprised, came to the house where I lived, waited outside for awhile, then came upstairs and knocked on my door. I was very startled, jumped out of bed, and thought only of getting ready as soon as I could. When I emerged fully dressed from my room, my friends fell back in manifest alarm. "What's that behind your head?" they cried. Since my awakening I had felt something preventing me from bending back my head, and I now groped for it with my hand. My friends, who had grown somewhat calmer, had just shouted "Be careful, don't hurt yourself" when my hand closed behind my head on the hilt of a sword. My friends came closer, examined me, led me back to the mirror in my room, and stripped me to the waist. A large, ancient knight's sword with a cross-shaped handle was buried to the hilt in my back, but the blade had been driven with such incredible precision between my skin and flesh that it had caused no injury. . . .

112

I don't believe people exist whose inner plight resembles mine; still, it is possible for me to imagine such people—but that the secret raven forever flaps about their heads as it does mine, even to imagine that is impossible.

[Next day] Eternal childhood. Life calls again.

Longing for the country? It isn't certain. The country calls forth the longing, the infinite longing.

Hesitation before birth. If there is a transmigration of souls then I am not yet on the bottom rung. My life is a hesitation before birth.

Kafka's Chief Works in English Translation

Most of these works and collections were published in book form posthumously. Dates given are for the first widely available publication, whether in German or English. The contents of some of the volumes of stories overlap.

The Hunger Artist and Other Stories (1924)*†
The Trial (1925)*†
The Castle (1926)*†
Amerika (1927)†
The Great Wall of China (1931)*

*starred entries indicate major works
†indicates work discussed in the text

KAFKA'S CHIEF WORKS

Description of a Struggle (1946)†
Wedding Preparations in the Country and Other Stories (1953)
Letter to His Father and Other Writings (1954)†
Metamorphosis and Other Stories (1961)* †

For Kafka's Diaries and Letters, see Recommended Reading.

Chronology of
Kafka's Life and Times

1883	Franz Kafka born July 3 in Prague, then part of the Austro-Hungarian Empire.
1893–1901	Attends German State Gymnasium (Altstadter Staatsgymnasium).
1901	Enters German University of Prague to study law.
1902	First meeting with Max Brod.
1903	First powered flight by the Wright brothers.
1906	Receives doctorate in law from German University of Prague.

1907	Employed by Assicurazioni Generali insurance company.
1908	Hired by Workers' Accident Insurance Institute for the Kingdom of Bohemia, a quasi-state organization.
1909	Visits Paris with Max Brod.
1912	Unsinkable *Titanic* strikes iceberg and sinks on maiden voyage. Meets Felice Bauer and begins voluminous correspondence with her.
1914	July: Kafka begins *The Trial*. Archduke Ferdinand of Austria assassinated in Sarajevo, precipitating outbreak of First World War. Kafka writes "In the Penal Colony."
1917	Bad health forces Kafka to begin taking intermittent sick leave from the Workers' Accident Insurance. Final break with Felice Bauer.
1918	First World War ends in defeat for Germany and Austro-Hungary. Collapse of Austro-Hungarian

Empire and creation of independent state of Czechoslovakia. Kafka writes *Letter to His Father*.

1919   Retires, with pension, from Workers' Accident Insurance Institute.

1920   Begins affair with Milena Jesenska-Polak.

1922   Last meeting with Milena. Begins writing *The Castle*. Writes "Investigations of a Dog."

1923   Kafka in Berlin with Dora Dymant.

1924   Kafka returns to Prague. Enters Sanitarium Kierling, near Vienna. Finishes story "Josephine the Singer." June 3, Kafka dies and is buried at the Prague-Straznice Cemetery. Kafka's collection of stories *The Hunger Artist* published in Leipzig.

1925   Max Brod organizes publication of *The Trial* in Germany.

1926   Publication of *The Castle*.

1933	Hitler comes to power in Germany and institutes first Nazi anti-Semitic laws. Kafka's works banned.
1937	Hitler annexes Czechoslovakia.
1939–1945	Second World War, during which Jewish culture in Central Europe is obliterated and its people exterminated. Death of Milena Jesenska-Polak and many of Kafka's relatives.
From 1945	Max Brod in Israel organizes publication and translation of remaining Kafka manuscripts.
1952	Death of Dora Dymant in London.

Recommended Reading

Max Brod, *Franz Kafka* (Da Capo Press, 1995). The first biography of Kafka, written by his closest friend. Gives a genuine feeling of what it was like to know Kafka and share his ideas during their time together in Prague and on holidays. A tendency to hagiography does not detract from this being a major document, which is filled with revealing insights into Kafka and how he regarded himself.

Ronald Hayman, *Kafka: A Biography* (Oxford University Press, 1982). A comprehensive literary biography by the major British biographer. It covers all aspects of Kafka's life from his works to the milieu of Prague, from his relationship with his father to his endless correspondence with Felice

and Milena. The book is consistently readable—
not always the case with works on Kafka—and
contains many psychological and philosophical
insights.

Gustav Janouch, *Conversations with Kafka* (New Directions, 1971). Here Kafka unburdens himself to
his young and admiring friend. Often they would
meet when Kafka had finished work, and Janouch
would copy down what they said together. This
must have been precisely how Kafka appeared to
his friends—a wise man of unique sensibility.

Franz Kafka, *Diaries 1910–1923* (Schocken, 1988).
These are endlessly intriguing and filled with
priceless snippets that illustrate Kafka's mind and
outlook, as well as innumerable false starts to un-
finished works and commonplace observations of
his daily habits. But the diaries should not be mis-
taken for the "real" Kafka, who appears in all his
finished glory only in his works.

Franz Kafka, *Letters to Felice* (Penguin, 1978). The
correspondence to end all correspondences, this
goes on for hundreds of pages, covering and re-
covering all of Kafka's neuroses and uncertainties. Here is an exceptional self-analyst being as
lucid as he can—though his motives for this self-
exposure are not quite so lucid.

Franz Kafka, *Letters to Milena* (Random House, 1999). This is a rather more sane correspondence, reflecting the sanity and forthrightness of the recipient of these letters. Unlike in his letters to Felice, you get the feeling that Kafka is addressing himself to his correspondent (at least most of the time). Here is Kafka trying to be normal, and none the worse for it.

Ernest Pawel, *The Nightmare of Reason: A Life of Franz Kafka* (Vintage Books, 1985). The most insightful and sympathetic modern study of Kafka. It contains many fascinating details as well as original ideas, but without descending into the farcical quagmire of interpretation that Kafka's work so often inspires in academic writers.

J. P. Stern, ed., *The World of Franz Kafka* (Holt, Rinheart and Winston, 1980). A selection of short essays by leading literary critics on many aspects of Kafka's life and work. It also has more than thirty illustrations of Prague, Kafka, and his family. Here you can see for yourself where it all happened—the picture takes on perspective as well as shadows.

Index

Werfel, Franz, 41
Workers' Accident Insurance Institute, 39, 97
Works: "The Aeroplanes at Brescia" (article), 43;
    Amerika, 49–57, 69; "The Burrow" (short
    story), 98; *The Castle,* 27, 90–97, 107–108;
    Description of a Struggle, 32–36; *Diaries,*
    110–113; "In the Penal Colony" (short story),
    84–89; "Josephine the Singer" (short story), 98;
    "Metamorphosis" (short story), 10, 21, 24, 49,
    57–64, 68, 69–70; *The Trial,* 27, 68–80, 81,
    84, 92, 95, 106–107, 111

Yiddish Theatre, 44, 92

A NOTE ON THE AUTHOR

Paul Strathern has lectured in philosophy and mathematics and now lives and writes in London. He is the author of the enormously successful series Philosophers in 90 Minutes. A Somerset Maugham Prize winner, he is also the author of books on history and travel, as well as five novels. His articles have appeared in a great many publications, including the *Observer* (London) and the *Irish Times*.

Paul Strathern's 90 Minutes series in philosophy, also published by Ivan R. Dee, includes individual books on Thomas Aquinas, Aristotle, St. Augustine, Berkeley, Confucius, Derrida, Descartes, Dewey, Foucault, Hegel, Heidegger, Hume, Kant, Kierkegaard, Leibniz, Locke, Machiavelli, Mars, J. S. Mill, Nietzsche, Plato, Rousseau, Bertrand Russell, Sartre, Schopenhauer, Socrates, Spinoza, and Wittgenstein.